CUT PAPER WORK

CUT PAPER WORK

BY CHRISTABEL RUSSELL COX

Formerly Lecturer in Art at the University of Birmingham

THE DRYAD PRESS

LEICESTER

PUBLISHED BY THE DRYAD PRESS

(DRYAD LIMITED)

PRINTED IN GREAT BRITAIN AT THE

CURWEN PRESS LTD., PLAISTOW

4TH IMPRESSION: 1951

THIS BOOK IS DEDICATED
WITH LOVE AND GRATITUDE TO
MY PARENTS

CONTENTS

LIST OF PLATES

FOREWORD

THE writing of a foreword to this book is not easy, for the author, in her admirable introduction, has said almost everything I should like to have said.

In the book itself she has shown in a very clear way the value of cut paper work as an educative process, and has explained how it can be adapted both to children of all ages and to students. She has, too, in an interesting and sound way shown how the subject should have a decisive character of its own and how the work can be made a valuable factor in stimulating a love of bold colour and sound decoration.

The fact that cut paper work gives a stimulus to all types of children makes it a valuable part of a fuller form of free expression work.

I can strongly recommend this book, for it is the result of many years of wide experience by a lecturer whose work, for its sincerity and power, has given me many years of great pleasure.

HAROLD H. HOLDEN

INTRODUCTION

THIS book has been written with a two-fold aim. In it I have endeavoured to illustrate and explain what I consider are the essential qualities of good cut paper work, and to suggest practical ways by which teachers can approach this kind of activity, either with classes of children or students, in order to give them both the ability to manipulate their materials and the enjoyment of expressing themselves in coloured paper work. These methods are not stunts. They do not inform the teacher how she can make her class produce untold marvels of achievement in the minimum amount of time. If they did, they would be useless both from the artistic and the educational standpoint. My experience, both with children of all ages and with students, has taught me that until people can control their scissors and paper they have neither the desire to express themselves by these means nor the ability to do so.

The degree of control that one expects naturally varies according to the age of the person who is using the materials, and the methods adopted by the teacher must obviously be less formal when dealing with a class of infants than with a class of children of nine or ten.

Paper cutting is an activity which has a strong appeal for both children and adults. The primary attraction is undoubtedly colour, but a medium which makes it possible to represent a shape directly, and not by the abstraction of an outline, has a special appeal for those who find drawing difficult.

The illustrations in this book (with the exception of Plates V, X, and XV) are not the work of children, but of students I have taught by the methods explained in the following chapters. These students in their turn have taught classes of children on the same methods suitably modified according to the particular ages they have to deal with.

If I were not confident of the soundness of these methods, which I have seen tested during the past seven years, this book would not have been written.

The illustrations are chosen frankly to give pleasure and to show what can be done in this attractive medium when its true qualities are appreciated. They illustrate the theories that the book propounds, but they are not meant as models to be copied, neither are they intended to represent the ability of the average person.

They are intended, however, to show how attractive cut paper work can be, and I hope they will serve their purpose in this way by encouraging my readers to venture in this medium. I also hope that they will find the methods I have suggested helpful in tackling the many practical problems which have to be faced.

ACKNOWLEDGEMENTS

I WISH to acknowledge, with gratitude, the help which many people have given me in the preparation and illustration of this book.

To Miss Bott, headmistress of Colmore Road Infant School, King's Heath, Birmingham, for lending me the originals of Plates V, X and XV.

To Fay Wainwright for lending me the original of Plate XX, and to the students whose work I have reproduced in addition to my own illustrations.

CHAPTER I

THE ESSENTIAL CHARACTER
OF GOOD CUT PAPER WORK

THE first thing one must recognize and understand when working with coloured paper and scissors, instead of with pencils and paints, is that here is a type of decoration which has very definite characteristics. Look at any piece of good work that has attracted you, and state in so many words where its attraction lies. Most people will say straight away, 'In the colour'. 'What else?' one may ask, for colour alone is not sufficient to give the amount of pleasure that one may derive from, say, Plate VIII in this book. You will probably next say that it is the shapes which attract you, and then, if you look still further, the arrangement of those shapes.

Good colour, good shape, and good arrangement—all these are qualities which must belong to good cut paper work. But I can hear people remark: 'They could equally well belong to any decorative design in any material,' and this is certainly true. These three qualities are necessary to any sound piece of artistic work. What, then, are the outstanding characteristics of cut paper work as distinct from, let us say, a drawn and painted decoration?

I think the answer lies in this. With a pencil and colours one can do almost anything within reason towards creating an illusion of reality in one's subject, for with a pencil one can define shapes, and with colour one can model those shapes in order to create an appearance of solid form on the flat paper. Moreover, one can add as much detail as one chooses to do, or as the subject at hand demands. Pencil and paints, in fact, are elastic media, imposing comparatively few restrictions on the user.

Compare these qualities with those of cut paper work. Scissors can define a shape definitely and satisfactorily, but no amount of skilful manipulation will create an appearance of convincing roundness or graduated form, and, if one struggles to attain these illusions, one loses the simple, bold character which is an essential charm of this particular type of work, in which definite shape and simplicity of detail are outstanding characteristics. In other words,(paper is definitely a flat material; one is using that material to make a decoration, not something that will satisfy one's sense of ingenuity or love of novelty and so lead one to say, 'How clever', or 'How real that looks'. Many people base their judgement of works of art on their realistic effect. In doing so they often forget to inquire whether it is the realism which gives them pleasure—that is to say, the craftsmanship of the artist—or whether it is the emotions that the object arouses which give them pleasure—that is, the inspiration of the artist, which has been so knit into his creation that it strikes an answering chord in the sympathetic admirer.

The qualities, then, which distinguish cut paper work most from other types of decorative work lie in the bold effect which is gained by sharply defined shapes harmoniously arranged, and by insistence on good flat shape rather than in striving to model to a seeming solidity which the material is ill-suited to express.)Many people will say that cut paper work has a poster-like quality. 'It stands out', they say; but they do not mean by this that it gives the appearance of realistic solid shapes standing out from a flat background, but refer simply to the bold effect of definite, flat, unmodelled shapes with the addition of comparatively little detail—another quality which the scissors soon make an obvious necessity when one starts to use them, for they are ill-suited to produce minute shapes.

As I have already remarked in my Introduction, this book has been written from a practical point of view in order to give help to teachers who are attracted by cut paper as a material, but find it difficult to

12

I. Trees and Crocuses (pastel and cut paper), by C. R. Cox

One-third actual size

II. Trees and Crocuses (pastel only)

One-third actual size

discover satisfactory methods of using it with classes of children. My practical outlook, however, does not in any way qualify or impede my appreciation of this work from the artistic point of view, and that is why I have spent the first part of this chapter in trying to define what I consider is the ideal to which one may attain in cut paper work. Unless one knows at what one is aiming little can be achieved; unless one respects the character of the material one works in, and the restrictions and limitations it imposes, one produces a hybrid type of work, a fusion of the qualities of one material with another, an ill-assorted marriage which destroys the good characteristics of both materials.

In this respect I am thinking of ways in which I have seen good cut paper work spoilt in schools by mixing it with other media. Sometimes this takes the form of shapes cut out of coloured paper, and stuck on to a pastel background, sometimes of whole figures or trees and other shapes drawn in pastel and cut out and applied to another background —either a coloured paper or a pastel one. In both these cases the results are almost equally bad.

To take the first case, that of putting coloured paper shapes on a pastel background (see Plate I). The effect of pastels is invariably soft in colour, it is never bold; and the most pleasing effects are gained by the delicate merging of colour which this material makes possible (cf. Plate II). Add to this natural soft quality the hard definiteness of cut paper shapes and you have a knife edge against a blunt one, a flat mass of brilliant colour against a texture which cannot pretend to rival the other in depth or strength of colour.

In the second case I refer to the cutting out of drawn shapes and applying them to a different ground—a thing which is frequently done in co-operative work. Generally, in order to procure these shapes, one is obliged to cut them out from the picture of which they were originally an integral part: a picture which has been composed individually by each child with every unit in it a part of that picture. That in itself is bad: to have to destroy one thing in order to create another.

Fig. 1. *Paper Crumpling*. Above: Sketch of model made by students, showing satisfactory use of paper crumpling for making vegetables and flowers. The pebbled path was made of balls of plasticine. Below: Detail of vegetables and sweet bottle filled with small crumpled paper balls for the sweet shop

I can hear teachers say, 'But the children like having things put into the co-operative picture. They don't mind having them cut out'. That, however, is not the point. You, as a teacher, should be giving children the opportunity of developing their taste and ability. When they make a pastel picture they should rightly take such a pride in doing it that they resent having it destroyed in order to create a co-operative picture from an assembly of their own as well as other people's drawings. You should be making the children more particular instead of less, and you are only defeating your own ends if you give way to the mere desire for recognition as opposed to the educational value of the work you should be doing, and the taste you should be educating. Moreover, this desire for recognition on the part of the child need in no way be thwarted, only in this particular application of the idea.

By all means let the children contribute to a co-operative cut paper picture, but let that picture be a unity of material, not a hybrid. Provide a cut paper background and let the children add cut paper figures and houses and trees, and you will be delighted with the result (see Plates VII and XV).

For illustration of this point I have included three illustrations of the same theme treated in different ways: one pure cut paper work (see Plate VII), one pure pastel work (see Plate II), and one a combination of the two materials (see Plate I). I leave you to judge as to when the materials are rightly used, having put forth my argument, and I feel little doubt as to what your final point of view will be.

Now another point arises here. Apart from the undesirability of cutting the contents from individual pictures in order to compose a co-operative picture, shapes drawn in pastel or in pencil and then coloured do not have the same effect as shapes cut direct from coloured paper.

Pastel and pencil and paints, as I have already remarked earlier in the chapter, allow for the introduction of far more and finer detail than cut paper work. Added to this, the hard edge given by the scissors to a

15

shape which has a softer effect of pastel or paint within its contours cannot stand up against shapes which are made directly in the surface colour: they look wrong, being neither units in a picture nor decorative shapes thought about in terms of cut paper, and the added detail within the drawn shapes looks fussy and out of place against the boldness and simplicity of directly cut masses.

Another type of misuse of coloured paper is of a different kind, and has its cause more than anything in a desire for novelty and an attempt to create an illusion of reality on one side, I think, and on the other to supplying an end for a very simple occupation for the children. I refer, in this case, to paper crumpling applied to pictures.

Paper crumpling can be used to excellent purpose in making a co-operative model. Here it is far more effective than flat paper shapes, which are just as much out of place in a model containing solid shapes as are solid shapes combined with flat paper. A model of a house can be supplied with flowers for the flower beds, roses for the walls of the house, blossom for the trees, vegetables for the vegetable garden, etc., and in recommending this usage I am including a sketch of a model made by students where crumpled paper has actually been used in these ways both attractively and satisfactorily (see Fig. 1). It is simply a question of finding a use for small, solid coloured shapes, and sweets, fruit, etc., for shops are another possibility when the house and garden have been exhausted, by which time the children will probably have developed beyond paper crumpling, and be capable of using scissors, for which exercise many suggestions will be found in the succeeding chapter.

A second departure from the essential flat use of the paper is often found in cases of flower cutting, where daffodils are the prime offenders.

Instead of getting the decorative effect by using a darker yellow for the trumpet than for the outer petals, and by taking a side view where the frilly edge of the trumpet is apparent, or as an alternative using a darker orange still for the inside of the trumpet if a three-quarter view is attempted (see Fig. 2 (right)), people are tempted to make a little cone of paper, which is gummed down on one edge to the background.

What does the picture gain by this? Is anyone convinced that this is a real daffodil?

Moreover, does it look any nicer than a trumpet, well shaped and stuck flat on the background? In departing from acceptance of the fact that one is making a flat decoration—in other words, a picture—when one should be employed in using good flat shapes in the best manner

Fig. 2. Left: Shape of petal and trumpet in side view of daffodil.
Right: Trumpet (two shapes required) in three-quarter view of daffodil.

possible, of what advantage is it to try to create an effect of realism by making shapes stand out solidly from the background? Remember, you are not playing a game of pretence; you are making something pretty: a decoration which will please your eye, not your sense of ingenuity and skill in forcing materials in directions which they do not want to follow, but something which will make your class-room look pretty and gay and cheerful.

Let me then sum up what I have tried to make clear in this chapter.

The characteristics of cut paper work which attract us are, primarily, its boldness and simplicity. In order to attain this boldness in its best form we must sacrifice desire for realistic effect, and substitute for this decorative effect. We must also sacrifice a large amount of detail which would be possible in a more elastic material, because our scissors limit us in this direction, and recognize that finickyness of over-fine detail harmonizes ill with the main, bold character of this type of material.

Ugly shapes in bold form are even more insistent on our notice than when they approach us in a less definite material, so the shapes we use must be good, and the colour of those shapes must be attractive.

Added to all this, colour and shape are of little avail if arrangement is poor, and here paper work stands us in good stead, for, unlike drawing, where one must delete before an alteration can be made, one can move one's shapes about until a satisfactory result is obtained.

In successive chapters these points are bound to recur, for they are the whole secret of the success of one's work in this attractive but definitely restricting medium—a medium which, I will add, is ill-designed for practical use, but for decorative purposes, when properly appreciated and handled, can produce most attractive results.

CHAPTER II

THE APPROACH TO THE CHILD IN THE INFANT SCHOOL AND EARLY JUNIOR CLASSES

ANY normal human being (and, for that matter, abnormal one, too) is attracted by gay or pleasant colour. Children in an infant school are most naturally no exception to this rule, since pleasure in colour is amongst our earliest appreciations. Nevertheless, economy has to be considered in schools, and I have found, from my experience, that although children of five and five-and-a-half may be attracted by coloured papers, they are incapable of producing anything very satisfactory, either to themselves or their teachers, until they can manage their scissors reasonably well, and as far as free cutting is concerned, until they have some sense of shape.

Consequently, until these qualities have developed to a certain extent, much waste will ensue if coloured cut paper work is attempted.

I have inferred in the previous chapter that cut paper work is definitely an art of the scissors and the paper.

I do not know whether my readers will have inferred from this that drawing should not be included in this type of work, but if they have not yet done so, I do mean to infer this, and will state my reasons.

Although it may possibly help an adult to define the shape he or she intends to cut by a line, I find that children derive no benefit from this method.

Even with adults, who have fine control of their fingers, and who are capable of visualizing a shape with relative accuracy, the use of the pencil can lead, unless great control is used, to more elaboration than the scissors are designed to perform. In the case of the child, whose sense of shape is not fully developed, and certainly not his standards of producing shapes, his control of the pencil is weak. Once a child has drawn a shape he will proceed to cut it out round his outline, no matter how poor and shaky that outline may be, or how unattractive the shape he has defined by that line. Moreover, I have never yet met a child who makes any effort to improve on his drawn shapes when he cuts them out! In other words, to produce a good shape, one should think in terms of making one shape from another—not in terms of following an outline round a shape, and I find children are remarkably capable at cutting shapes directly in the paper, whereas, if allowed to draw the shape first, their attempts are small, meagre and ill-controlled.

Infants of five, unless they come from a home where they have been able to use scissors and to indulge in cutting out, can frequently do little but snip with the scissors, and even this action is irregular and uncertain.

It would obviously, therefore, be unwise to plan a scheme of work until the children have got used to their scissors, and for this first exercise of snipping, the co-operative model often finds a purpose, chopping up little pieces of straw for the ground of the cornfield, or of green raffia for grass, or of coloured paper for confetti if a wedding is made the subject of a model. Leading from this, fringing of mats naturally follows on, where, in addition to snipping with the scissors, an effort is being made to make the cuts of the same length; and, after this, toothing the edges of paper presents the further difficulty of cutting alternately at two different angles. (See Fig. 3).

Best of all, however, to give children real joy in the control of their scissors, nothing is better than making a scrap book.

Nature is in many ways a kindly, sensible body. She does not, as we teachers tend to do, rush people on from one thing to another before they are ready to make the change. 'One thing at a time', she says, and until a child can use his scissors happily and easily without their bothering him, she keeps him content to cut just for the sake of cutting, taking a pride in his achievement as he gradually cuts better and better. If only teachers would realize this, what a lot of bother they would save

20

themselves in thinking out all sorts of lessons which are far too difficult for the children and result simply in a waste of paper; whereas fashion books, bulb catalogues, advertisements of a suitable and attractive nature—not to mention remains of dismembered picture books—provide ample and inexpensive material and invaluable experience.

Even just cutting out, however, needs to be graded in difficulty if the children are going to get full benefit from this exercise. Cutting round elaborate shapes means that the scissors must be manipulated at different angles, and until a child can cut easily and well in one direction with some control, he cannot change the action in time to follow the intricacies of a figure in a fashion book.

In order to give the children something which they are capable of doing reasonably well, within scope of their ability, I find it is advisable to let them cut out whole pictures first, where cutting along a straight line with care develops the control which will stand them in good stead when they come to more difficult exercises. The teacher must watch the development of this control, for it will not come with one or two lessons, and the lessons must be short, for small fingers soon tire.

In these lessons a certain portion of the time should definitely be allotted to both cutting and to sticking down. So often the latter exercise is squeezed in with a rush at the end of the lesson, and consequently very badly done, and in learning control of materials, pasting and sticking presents a valuable exercise. Newspaper should be supplied to each desk, and the children should be directed to smooth over their pasted picture with a clean sheet of paper when they apply it to the page of their book. Bad workmanship in this type of work is just what the teacher wants to avoid, for she is laying the foundation of habits which will cling long after facts and figures are forgotten.

Moreover, so much handwork presents real difficulty to children, and here is an exercise which can be done well, when care and pride in work is encouraged, by even the more clumsy child. I should say that at least one-third of the lesson should be allotted to arranging and

Fig. 3. (1) Fringing. (2) Toothing. (3) Toothing and also folding and cutting. (4) Folding and cutting strings of figures (Teacher outlines shape on first fold).

sticking down, and each child should be allowed to make his own scrap book if the full benefit is to be derived from this exercise, for the personal possession means so much. It is a good plan to make the pages of separate folded sheets each lesson, and then finally assemble them, for, if a page is spoilt or too much paste is used, it can be discarded without spoiling the whole book, whereas, if a book is used in the first place, there is always the danger of the pages getting stuck together through over-generosity in the application of paste.

5

Fig. 3—*continued*   (5) Free cutting of shapes of clothes for washing day.

Teachers often ask me if I advise them to cyclostyle shapes for the children to cut out in order to make friezes for the class-room. If this is definitely the aim, and the children are still at a stage when they are best occupied in cutting round lines, I do think this exercise suitable, but teachers must discriminate in the type of shapes they choose. These should be clear silhouettes, not just any drawings traced on to coloured paper and quite incomprehensible without the drawn details within their contours.

Drawing round shapes and letting the children fill them in with crayon afterwards and cutting them out to make a frieze is an exercise which I heartily condemn. Coloured paper friezes always look gay, even if the shapes are not too good, but smudgy pastel shapes always look dingy, no matter how well they are done, and when children can

23

do an exercise like this well enough for it to look even doubtfully well done, they could be better occupied in far more intelligent ways.

Now, when a child is reasonably proficient, through simple cutting exercises, in the use of his scissors, other kinds of work can be introduced.

Some of my readers may think that I have rather contradicted myself in this chapter. First I say that no drawing should be allowed in conjunction with cut paper work, and then I suggest that infants should be set to cut round drawings. I admit that this sounds like a contradiction, but in reality it is not so.

The attitude of mind in which one sets out to define a shape by a line and then to cut it out is quite different from that of a small child cutting out a picture.

In one case the aim is to produce a shape which one begins by defining by a line; in the other, it is merely to develop dexterity in the control of the scissors by following lines which frequently change their direction.

As the children gain in dexterity with their scissors in their cutting lessons through practical exercise, so, in their drawing lessons, through the frequent use of their chalks or crayons or paints to express their experiences in visual form, their sense of shape will develop, and consequently, by the time they have learnt to use their scissors properly, they will have other material for expression on which they can draw.

Shapes for first lessons in free cutting should be bold and simple, and washing day provides a most suitable and enjoyable subject.

The children can begin by cutting two posts as long as their paper will take, and sticking them in position, one at each end of the paper. The straight edge of the paper can serve as a guide in keeping the lines as even as possible, and the clothes line itself can be cut as thin as the children can manage it, and attached to the posts. This will probably have to be cut in two halves or in three parts and joined, as the work must be on a reasonably large scale or it is too finicky for the children to manage. (See Fig. 3).

24

If this line is drawn in chalk, it may be thinner, but it looks faint and out of place in contrast with the boldness of the coloured paper (see first chapter *re* mixing of materials).

The enjoyment of this lesson will be considerably increased if, whilst the children are cutting their clothes lines, the teacher puts up her line across the classroom, and then proceeds to hang up garments one by one as the children progress.

If all the garments are hung up simultaneously, much of the dramatic development of the lesson is lost, as each fresh article can provide new interest, and also gives scope for a very short pause in which observations are made, whereas if all the garments are hung up at once, the children will probably get very excited, whilst their aim will be to gallop through the whole lot of shapes as rapidly as possible in order to complete the picture, regardless of any care in the carrying out of the work!

I know that large numbers present the difficulty of different rates at which different children work, but nevertheless, this method is by far the most satisfactory that I have discovered in combining action and instruction.

When children are beginning free cutting, if they have little sense of shape, a variety of garments for washing day would present many difficulties, and a jolly lesson can be made from a handkerchief wash-day when some family has been ill with colds!

This provides excellent practice in cutting square shapes, which can be of different colours and different sizes for various members of the family, and by sticking a smaller square inside a larger one, a handkerchief with a coloured border will result.

It is always best to let the children practise first on rough paper. This saves a lot of waste of more expensive coloured paper, and also it helps to make the children realize that care must be taken and that they cannot use their coloured paper until they have really tried and shown what they can do.

Garments that are suitable for a general washing day can include handkerchiefs, pillow-cases, jersey, knickers, scarf, socks, etc., and the more colourful the better. If on one day a teacher should want to give particular experience in cutting out shapes of dresses, a frock washing day could be indulged in, and different coloured dresses cut out and hung up. Of necessity, the shapes of dresses which are obtainable to hang up are generally rather floppy and flimsy, which presents some difficulty in determining a shape. If a teacher is judicious in doing so, she might sometimes cut the shapes out on a large scale, and build up her picture with those of the children, but she must realize in doing this that she is making the aim of her lesson a technical one rather than that of expression, and as long as she realizes this and allows expression later on, all well and good.

This might be done in the following way. Assuming that several lessons have been taken on cutting clothes, the teacher might begin her lesson by saying: 'Now, some weeks ago we pretended to have a hand-kerchief washing day, and we cut out different coloured square shapes for handkerchiefs and hung them on the line we had cut. Another time we washed dresses, and another time we washed all sorts of clothes for the family.

'This time you can decide what kind of a wash-day you will have—a handkerchief wash because your family have had colds, or a general wash because it is Monday, or a frock washing day because you and your sisters are going to a party, and you can cut out just what clothes you like, and hang them up on your clothes line, but don't forget, if you decide to have a general wash, and do Daddy's overalls that he wears at work, or a pair of his trousers, that they must be bigger than the ones you hang up for yourself, or else it will look as though all the people in your family are the same size!'

Another time a teacher might want to encourage cutting of figures, which, in coloured paper, must be built up shape by shape. This could begin by the cutting of a dress or jersey and trousers and adding a head, hands, legs, hair, etc., afterwards.

26

In a first lesson of this type, some definite direction is needed, and the action should again be divided into stages.

In an expression lesson, growing out of the experience gained in the more formal lesson, a subject such as 'The gym. tunic I should like to have' for the girls, or 'A football outfit I should like' for the boys, will serve as a nucleus to a picture, or can be made a picture in itself.

Here, of course, the children would work freely and unrestrainedly, using whatever experience they have gained in the previous more formal lessons, whilst the teacher should be available for help or advice when needed.

This same method can be adopted also in the cutting of toys, which always provide attractive subject matter—a ship, a bat and ball, a gollywog, a doll, or a doll's house, are all suitable as long as their shapes are good and simple. In each of these cases the toy is, of course, built up of a number of shapes, and as the toy is built up, so the cut paper picture must be made.

The children can then, if they like, pretend that they are making the toys, and consider what shape piece of wood, for instance, they would need to make the boat itself. 'What shaped piece of wood do you need for this part of the boat?' 'A long, rather narrow piece.' 'Let us cut that first then, in our rough paper. Now, what are we going to do to this to make it like the boat in shape?' The answer will be, in all probability, 'Chop off the ends, Miss!'

'Yes, but how shall we chop them off? Are the two ends of the boat the same shape? Stop and look what this shape does; first it slopes in to the keel, and then the keel slopes out again.' This fact might be emphasized by drawing the direction of the two lines on the board, and getting the children to move their hands in the direction of the lines to get the feel of the shape. Then the other end can be done. After this, the masts can be cut. 'Are they as tall as the boat is long?' 'Mind you put them in the right place on the boat', etc.

27

Next, of course, come the sails, and so the whole toy can be assembled and eventually stuck down.

I have seen lessons taken in this way with top classes in an infant school with great success. Proportion, of course, is not stressed, but it can be referred to quite naturally, and the children then left to see how much they can observe and register in their practical work.

Co-operative lessons can follow quite naturally, too, from these toy-cutting lessons; but they bring up an entirely new set of problems which I will deal with in a succeeding chapter.

III. Flower Cutting (purple and green), by Hilda Wellings

Two-thirds actual size

IV. Flower Cutting (purple and green), by J. L. Cowley

Three-quarters actual size

CHAPTER III

COLOUR

IN dealing with the question of colour, it is obvious that success depends on the stock of material which the teacher selects. Unless the colour is attractive, I consider cut paper work a waste of time from the artistic point of view. The actual cutting, even in ugly colours, will, of course, afford opportunity for developing manipulative skill, but it is a poor and depressing business to work in this way.

I find that most of the trouble with colour in schools arises from the fact that teachers requisition for packets of selected colours, rather than colours selected by themselves. The invariable result is that all the attractive colours are used up in the first lessons and then, for economical reasons, the remainder has to be finished!

It is at this stage that brilliant pink and a rather sickly mauve make their appearance round the class-room walls, together with an ugly dark brownish red!

The results are horrible!

I must, therefore, try to persuade my readers to buy their colours in a different way.

The Dryad Handicrafts stock an excellent selection of coloured papers, which can be bought by the quire or by individual sheets, either with or without gummed backs, as preferred.

Those of my readers who have been studying the Ostwald Colour Theory will find amongst these papers a range, firstly, of fulltone colours or hues; secondly of tints (that is, these hues lightened with white); and thirdly, of shades (that is, the same range of hues darkened and made duller by the inclusion of black). When confronted by such a range of attractive colour, it will probably be difficult to make a selection unless it is done systematically and, from my own experience, the most satisfactory method is this.

C

29

With a class of fifty children, or even with such a comparatively small number as thirty, because of the numerous problems that arise, it is impossible to allow individual choice of colour when beginning cut paper work, and the only alternative, from the artistic standpoint, is for the teacher herself to select colour that is gay and attractive.

I would suggest that, at first, the children's work should be carried out with a limited range of fulltone hues, and a stock laid in of these particular colours. The tints and shades can be added to stock gradually, and as skill in the manipulation of cutting shapes develops, more time can be given to the selection of more elaborate colour schemes.

In any case, the most attractive work is almost invariably produced with a limited range of colours and, if the coloured illustrations in this book are studied, it will be seen that there is not a large colour range used in any one individual picture.

So many people are worried when confronted with the problem of selecting a colour scheme that I think the adoption of a half-humorous simile will help to make this easier. The primary colours are individuals, possessing individual qualities—these are Yellow, Red, and Blue, and the fusion of these in pairs will produce, in turn, Orange, Green, and Purple.

The idea of fusion links up colours with individual people and family life: Yellow marries Red and produces a child—Orange. A greater proportion of one or other colour results in a child with characteristics belonging to one parent rather than the other, and so we can have red orange or yellow orange! This establishes the idea of colour families, which is a less formidable way of speaking of colours than by referring to them as harmonies. The full-tone colour family which produces the most gay and attractive results in cut paper work is, I think, the Yellow-to-Red family, and I should advise teachers to lay in a good stock of yellow, orange yellow, orange, red orange, scarlet and, on the green side, yellow green, green, and blue green as a beginning. Later on, she may add the blue and purple range of hues to her stock.

30

This means that she does not stock too large a quantity of individual hues, but aims at giving experience with different families in turn, first Yellow to Red, then Red to Purple, etc.

The first work with the children can be carried out in two colours for the flowers—one colour for the flower shapes and a smaller quantity of a second colour for their centres, and either one or two greens for the stems and leaves.

As the children proceed to the use of two or more types of flower in a study, the range of colours used can be extended—say yellow with orange-yellow centre for one flower, the reverse colour scheme for a second, whilst a third can be in scarlet with orange centre, and the scarlet flowers can have blue-green leaves.

The detail of centres to the flowers is one which demands care and consideration. Many otherwise good pieces of work are often spoilt because the child or student tends to think of each flower individually instead of as a part of the whole colour design, and adds a centre, which, considering the flower individually, looks satisfactory, but when added to the group proves either too insipid or too violent in contrast.

It is wiser to cut and arrange the flowers loosely on the paper, and then judge where it will be helpful to include the colour of one flower in another, and where to add contrast of tone or hue.

The story of colour families can be extended when the question of introducing contrast arises.

A contrasting colour, as I expect my readers know, is one taken from the directly opposite side of the colour circle; for instance, the contrast to yellow is blue, not a greenish-blue or a purplish-blue, but what we tend to think of as Reckitt's blue. The contrast to scarlet is blue-green, to reddish purple yellow-green. The true contrasts, that is of colours diametrically opposed, can be worked out by reference to any reliable colour circle, but any colours from the opposite side of a colour circle included in a prevailingly harmonious scheme will give a contrasting

31

effect, for instance, the inclusion of blue in a prevailing scheme of yellow, orange, and red. (See Plate IX).

To return, however, to our colour families and the similes they make conveniently possible. Generally speaking, families agree pretty well together—their relationship to one another creates a harmony, but even the happiest families, and the most self-contained, welcome a visitor sometimes to brighten things up and to make a change! That is what a contrast does to a prevailing colour scheme—gives it that little sparkle of change which prevents monotony.

Nevertheless, we all know the effect produced by a guest who outstays his or her welcome! Too much of the nicest visitor's company is apt to pall, and so, in a colour scheme, too much of the contrasting colour is apt to upset the equilibrium of the colour harmony: the family's tastes get overborne by those of the visitor!

Therefore, in using a contrasting colour in a scheme, it should only be introduced in small quantities—for the smallest flowers, which should not be grouped together in large quantities, or for the centres of some of the other flowers.

The only way in which one's sense of colour can develop is through the use of colour, and through experience in the use of different colours and the effect of their combination in different quantities. Different effects can be produced by the predominance in proportion of each colour in turn of a certain range. For instance, in a red-orange-yellow colour scheme, if the largest flowers are made red, orange, and yellow respectively in three respective pieces of work, the results will be totally different.

Consequently, when the first difficulties of cutting have been passed over, the teacher can give the class individual choice as to which colour they would like for their largest flowers, and so individuality will come into the work.

I have not mentioned, so far, the inclusion of tints, that is, paler versions of the full tones or hues—or shades—that is, the darkened or

V. Cockyolly Birds. Colmore Road Infant School, John Rees (aged 6+)

Half actual size

VI. Toy Shop, by group of students

One-quarter actual size

dullened hues—into the colour range. These, I think, should be introduced as extras to a prevailing colour scheme to provide further interest as experience grows. It will generally be discovered that the shades, or dullened hues, are of great benefit to the bright gay hues, in preventing these from being garish, whilst the tints do much to prevent the darkened hues, such as purple and blue, from looking too heavy and dull as a prevailing colour scheme.

One range of colours I have omitted to mention so far, mainly in order to prevent confusion, is the range of colours referred to by Ostwald as the 'greyed shades'. Actually, I think 'greyed tints' would be a more explicable term to most people, since those who are familiar with a water-colour box are more apt to think of making colours paler by the addition of water than by the addition of white paint. The 'greyed shades' are the fulltone hues with the addition of both black and white, giving the effect of the inclusion of a little black to the colour of the tints.

These greyed shades, i.e., fawn, dull pink, pale dull blue or mauve, etc., are sometimes far more effective than the clearer tints or darker shades as an addition in a colour scheme.

Now I have referred to the enlivening effect of contrasting colour in a prevailing colour scheme. I would point out that there is another way of producing contrasting effects, and that is by the addition of contrasts of tone.

Every colour has a tone relation, that is, a relative degree of lightness or darkness to every other colour. Yellow, for instance, is the palest-toned colour in the colour circle. A fulltone yellow cannot be made any darker but by the addition to it of another colour, which will change both its hue and tone. For instance, the addition of a little blue to yellow, which is of a considerably darker tone than yellow itself, produces a green-yellow which is darker than the original pure yellow in tone. Sometimes the effect of a contrast of hue in a colour scheme presents an effect which is more startling than is wanted, and here the inclusion of either a small quantity of a pale tint or a dark shade will serve the purpose of relief from monotony with a quieter result.

This is called a contrast of tone.

In concluding, however, I would say that it is no guarantee that careful adherence to the strictest colour theory will necessarily produce beautiful colour, because, given beautiful coloured materials to use, the results can be surprisingly disappointing unless the question of relative quantity has been sensitively realized. Some people are born with an instinctive sense of colour, and will always produce work of an individual charm and attraction because they can sense, without bothering about any rules, just what colour they need to complete a certain scheme. For the rest, though, who find it very difficult sometimes to discover just why a piece of work has not got the unity it needs, I would point out that the success of the colour in attractive work lies mainly in the fact that the shapes used are not all of the same size and, therefore, quantity of colour. The colours need to graduate in importance in the colour scheme: one colour must dominate or lead the other colours in the same way as the family is dominated by the head of the family.

Looking at a colour scheme where every colour quantity is equal, is like trying to listen to a room full of people all talking at once, which produces a confusion of meaning and of sound. The easiest way to ensure harmony is to choose which colour one wishes to dominate, and cut the largest flowers from this. The colour next in importance, then, should be cut in the next largest size, and so on (see Plate XII).

From the point of view of shape, again, it is unwise to make every flower equally important. If all the flowers have curved petals the effect is monotonous; if they are all indented the effect is fussy and restless, but a combination of a rather elaborate cornflower type of flower, such as that produced by cutting three 'V' shapes from a petal, with a smooth round-petalled flower of a slightly smaller size, is much more pleasing.

34

It is always difficult to speak of colour without examples to illustrate points, because theory is so very confusing without practice, unless one is very experienced and can visualize what is being said. It is not possible, due to the expense it would entail, to illustrate all the points about which I have spoken, but a careful reference to the coloured plates will help to make my meaning clear.

CHAPTER IV

THE CUTTING OF FLOWER SHAPES

ONE of the essential things to realize in teaching art of any kind is that here is a practical lesson in which the class should be doing practical work, not listening to a lecture as to how that practical work can and should be carried out.

I should imagine that one of the worst and most common mistakes made in the teaching profession is the failure to realize that, by trying to forestall and prevent the making of mistakes, one is destroying both the power of initiative in the children and a sound foundation of interest on which instruction can be based for the teacher. Nobody who has taught practical work can deny that the instinct of the class is to be doing, not listening. The number of times one hears the phrases, 'No, I do not want you to start yet', 'No, put your scissors down and listen to me', etc., testifies to this.

Now this may appear to infer that I do not agree with preliminary instruction, but I do not mean this at all.

What I do mean, however, is that the teacher should not try to do all her instruction in the first ten minutes of the lesson to a class unwilling to sit and listen, for not only does she begin with the children in the wrong frame of mind, but her instructions will not be fully attended to and will have to be repeated again later in the lesson, by which time they will have lost their freshness.

What, then, is the alternative? Obviously to divide the action into stages which can give opportunity for experiment, instruction, and the carrying out of those instructions, whereby a class will be doing practical work nearly the whole time.

This method is in reality very like the Æsop's fable of trying to break the bundle of sticks, which, it will be remembered, was impossible to

36

VII.   Trees and Crocuses, by C. R. Cox.   (One-third actual size).

VIII. Posy, by Mavis Brown. (Two-thirds actual size).

IX. Garland, by group of students. (Quarter actual size).

X. A Little Girl in a Garden. After child aged 7+. Colmore Road Infant School. (Half actual size).

XI. Spring, by E. Price. (Half actual size).

XII.   The Effect of Varying Relative Quantities of Colour, by C. R. Cox.   (Half actual size).

XIII. Christmas Tree, by C. R. Cox. (One-third actual size).

XIV. Spring Flower Frieze, by C. R. Cox. (Half actual size).

snap in half when attacked collectively, but, by dealing with the sticks one by one, the difficulty was eventually resolved! To illustrate this method, I have included plans of lessons in a succeeding chapter, but in this chapter I intend to talk about how one can teach the actual cutting of flower shapes to children or students who are capable of free cutting.

I have already discussed in the chapter on the essential characteristics of paper cutting, how drawing is more of a hindrance than a help in this type of work, so that the use of the pencil will not enter into the discussion.

In my experience I have found that there has been little necessity to alter the main method of teaching free cutting of flowers with either juniors or seniors, or students. The difference occurs in the rate at which the children become capable of producing good work, and of tackling the cutting of gradually more intricate shapes.

I do not find it advisable to embark on a course of flower cutting with juniors younger than nine years of age, and preferably nine plus to ten years, because the patience and skill demanded in producing good shapes is apt to worry the younger children, and I feel they are better cutting shapes such as toys and making pictures freely which depend less on symmetry for beauty of effect. I do not hold to this as a hard and fast rule, but generally speaking I advise it.

Apart from this, children in the lower part of the junior school are still almost unanimously keen on expressing themselves through drawing, of which, as they grow older and develop in power of criticism, they begin to fight shy and are, therefore, all the more ready to try their hand in other decorative fields.

It is just as well not to take the edge off the children's appetites by introducing sooner than necessary an activity which will fit in better with their ability and interest at a later date.

When I first became attracted to paper cutting, I assumed that it would be an easy thing to produce flower shapes by free cutting without any definite system, but lamentable failure both in my teaching of students and children led me to the decision that either I must resort to using pencil drawing (which I felt sure was wrong—for if one was going to draw the shape, why not paint it too instead of bothering with pieces of coloured sticky paper?) or abandon paper work as not worth the trouble.

My admiration for the work produced in Austria by Professor Cizek's children's class vetoed the latter of these two conclusions, for if they could do it, why could not we? I therefore set to work to evolve a system whereby beautiful flowers could be produced by cutting shape from shape, and from my practical experience, developed a method which I have seen adopted satisfactorily by numerous students over a period of years, and by many classes in their charge.

Before I explain this method, I should like to make one observation as to why I begin by cutting conventional flowers instead of working from real flowers. To many people I know this would appear wrong, as though I were putting the cart before the horse, but here we must go back to an observation I made in the chapter on the essential character of this medium. Cut paper is a decorative medium — it is ill-suited to naturalistic representation—and an inexperienced child or adult finds it an extremely difficult task to select the decorative features most suited to representation in paper cutting. Later, when they have learnt the decorative possibilities of the medium through cutting conventional shapes, they are more capable of making this selection.

If one studies flowers, it is obvious that their difference one from the other consists in their colour, their general shape—which may be either circular or of the bell variety—and in the number, shape and arrangement of their petals, and it is on this that I have based my methods of cutting.

We will start by considering flowers which are based on a circle, and obviously the first essential is to be able to cut a circle, so this provides the first and immediate exercise.

38

To begin with, the class can experiment with rough paper, and, of course, there is always a number of people who fold their paper in two or in four and then attempt to cut either a semicircle or a segment.

This method almost invariably produces a shape which is either oval (see Fig. 4 (right)) or scalloped (see Fig. 4 (left)), since, until it is unfolded, the true shape is not visible.

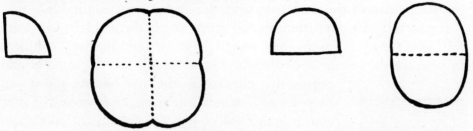

Fig. 4. Results of folding and cutting to obtain a circle

Other children will cut directly into a sheet of paper and produce a reasonably good circle, but without any planning of the shape, and a good deal of paper is wasted. This does not matter with rough paper, but it certainly will with coloured paper, which must be dealt with economically.

Occasionally one will find a child who has a sufficiently constructive mind to cut a square, and then cut a circle from it—a method which is the most satisfactory that I have found. If there is found a child who has done this, then his work can be used as an illustration, but failing this the teacher can demonstrate—the cutting of a square, and then, beginning from the middle of the side of the square, the curving-off of the corners (Fig. 5).

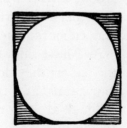

Fig. 5.
Correct method of
cutting a circle

The demonstration in paper, with scissors, can be emphasized by a drawing on the board, and the class can go back to work.

People might think that it is being unnecessarily fussy not to let the children draw circles, either with compasses or around coins. I have tried this as a method, and find that invariably the same thing happens —that they take the line of least resistance and start drawing in their shapes with the pencil and, as a result, do not cut nearly so well. Moreover the use of coins to provide circles limits the children to the particular size of the available coin, which may be unsuitable.

It generally takes a little time, however, to get the children to realize the use of the square as an enclosure to the circle, and they will continue to produce the results indicated by Fig. 6, unless this is patiently and persistently checked in the first lessons, for it can be pointed out how much paper is wasted if they continue to cut like Fig. 6, whereas the minimum is cut away when working in the proper way, and more important still, the square is a definite guide in the cutting of the circle.

Fig. 6.
Child's method of cutting a circle

Once the problem of the circle has been tackled (and simple circular flowers with different coloured circles in the centre are very effective as a beginning) the easiest division of the circle to attempt is the four-petalled flower.

I am not going to discuss in detail the methods of procedure of the lesson, as this will be dealt with in another chapter. Suffice it to say that, before instruction is given, there should always be opportunity and encouragement to experiment.

As I have said, the inexperienced, when cutting a circle, tend to fold the paper; they do the same thing when trying to divide the circle into four petals, and this is a bad method.

There are two reasons why I so strongly object to folding the paper. In the first place, creases in the paper spoil the freshness and beauty of effect and, in the second place, they reduce what should be an exercise in developing sensitiveness to beauty of shape to something

40

XV. Postman Scene. Children at Colmore Road Infant School (aged 5+ to 6)

One-quarter actual size

XVI. Flower Design, by a group of students

One-third actual size

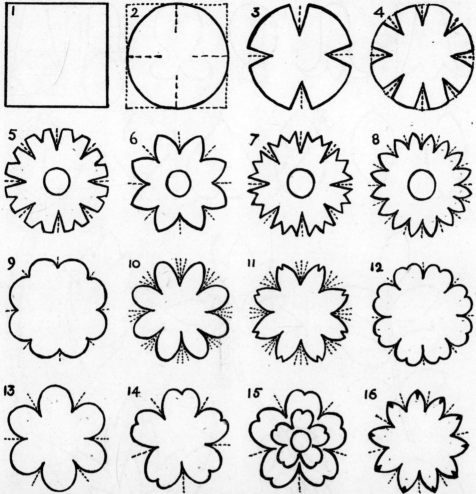

Fig. 7. The shapes illustrated above show how the circular shape is cut from a square and then divided into four petals, then eight, which can be decorated by cutting out a small V-shape, or two V-shapes as in No. 7. Since this is more intricate to cut, the pointed petals, as in No. 6, might be attempted as a previous exercise. No. 8 shows sixteen-pointed petals, No. 9 rounded petals. It will be noticed that in some cases, as in No. 9, that after cutting the dividing slits, the V-shaped division can be omitted; (cf. with No. 10) which tends to give a more solid flower. Nos. 13 and 14 show divisions of six and five petals respectively, Nos. 15 and 16 decorative treatments of centres and petal edges

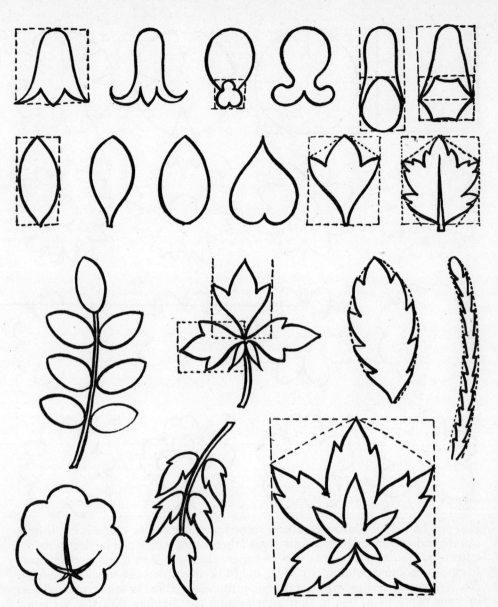

Fig. 8. Bell-shaped flowers and simple and compound leaves—methods of cutting

entirely mechanical where the whole shape is not visible whilst it is being cut. Under these circumstances, how can one expect to produce a beautiful shape? Moreover, one cannot fold for multiples of three; so how can such a method help when one wants to cut six or twelve-petalled flowers? So much depends in this kind of work on sensitiveness to beauty of shape, and good judgement of eye and hand, that one should adopt methods where these faculties are called into play. The solution of the difficulty of even division is so simple that one wonders why one did not think of it immediately. Obviously, if the scissors are the instrument, cutting should be substituted for folding!

A slit cut with the scissors pointing directly towards the centre is the first step. Then, by turning the circle round so that the slit is at the top of the circle, and cutting a slit of similar length directly opposite, the circle is divided into two but still remains joined. A further slit of the same length midway between these slits, and one opposite to it, produces four equal divisions.

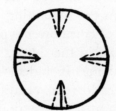

Fig. 9. Necessity of pointing scissors towards centre

Care should be taken always to point the scissors directly towards the centre of the circle, of course, or the symmetry of the shape will be spoilt (see Fig. 9). After cutting the slits, a small segment is cut away from each side of the slit, and the result is a four-petalled flower.

This, of course, is the nucleus of the whole system, and once this simple exercise has been mastered satisfactorily, eight divisions are the next easiest to attempt.

The cutting of six- twelve- five- and ten-petalled flowers involves skill in sense of judgement of space—a skill which juniors, at all events, are not capable of acquiring very soon, and therefore, having mastered

43

the division of the circle into four and eight, the next stage I advise is to turn the interest to the shaping of the petals.

The floral shapes illustrated in this chapter have been arranged in sequence of difficulty of cutting.

I find that, when the teaching of shaping of petals is attempted by inexperienced teachers, they almost invariably choose the rounded petal.

Actually, I find, myself, that the round shape demands far more skill of control than the more elaborate looking shapes, which are decorated by indentations.

These simply involve cutting a 'V' shape from the centre of the petal, for which a tiny guide slit can be made first, as in the dividing up of the circle, and a small segment cut from each side of the slit. A similar shape cut from the remaining two divisions of the petals gives the effect of a flower of cornflower type, or the simple pink, according to the number of petals in the shape.

A study of the drawings included with this chapter will go further towards making my readers conversant with the possibilities of different shapes than any amount of instructions, for when I have said that the flower shapes illustrated in this chapter are arranged in order of general difficulty of cutting, it remains for them to experiment and find out how far this applies to them. (See Figs. 7 and 8).

I have here dealt with methods of cutting the floral shapes—one of the essential characteristics of good cut paper work of this type.

In the next chapter I will discuss the question of arrangement, which constitutes the remaining outstanding attraction.

CHAPTER V

FLOWER ARRANGEMENT

I HAVE now discussed the question of cutting in order to produce good shape, and also that of colour selection and quantity. In this chapter on arrangement, I want to refer not only to possibilities of arrangement, but also to ways in which one can gradually make children and students conscious of the necessity of some degree of symmetry and balance. In the same way as I would begin each practical lesson by letting the children start cutting straight away, I would begin the question of arrangement by letting the children plan and stick down their work, making all the mistakes which I expect them to make first, rather than, by enumerating all these possibilities of error, hold them back from broadening their experience by the more gradual process of progressive improvement.

In a first lesson the children have begun, we will assume, by experimenting in cutting circles, followed probably by a demonstration of how this can be done by the teacher. From this comes the progression to experiment in cutting four-petalled flowers and, if necessary, the teacher's demonstration. The flowers have then to be cut in coloured paper, and also some leaves and stems.

If, when the children come to arranging their flowers, the teacher holds them back from achieving the culmination of their activity, they will be restless and, very naturally, disinclined to listen. The wise teacher will suggest that, having cut their flowers and leaves, they have now got to arrange them and stick them down, which they must do carefully to make them look as pretty as possible, just as they would take care in arranging them if they were real and if they had picked them in order to give them to someone. She will then leave the children to produce what they may. It is always best, in first lessons, to let the children make a small, complete posy of the few flowers they have cut rather than to save these and add to them in another lesson in order to make a more elaborate piece of work.

In these first lessons, where the problems of cutting are being tackled, there will not be sufficient flowers produced to fill a pot or vase effectively, so it is best to adopt the plan of making posies, and go on to making bigger groupings when the children have a greater number of flower shapes in their repertoire, and there is not the necessity of learning new shapes, which absorbs so much time in the lesson. It is always a wise plan for the teacher to give each child an envelope into which she can put any flowers not wanted, or scraps of odd colours too small to collect for the 'bit box', which every practical teacher will keep in which to store odd pieces of paper too big to be considered waste. Both these stores will provide material when small quantities of colour are needed for centres of flowers, etc., and it will inculcate orderly habits in the classroom in the management of materials.

The results in arrangement of the children's first lesson provide excellent material for the basis of a second lesson, which may be for the purpose of revising the work of the last lesson and of considering arrangement and finding out the different possibilities in this direction.

The accompanying diagrams (see Fig. 10) will show some of the typical mistakes which the children will make in their first pieces of work. They are naturally anxious to see what the flowers look like stuck down, and there are nearly always some children who, in their haste, forget that flowers grow so that the heads hide the stalks where they join. These children will stick the flowers down first and then have the difficult problem of fitting in their stems!

Few children will consider the shape that their collection of flowers will make, and the results of their arrangements will vary from a wide, irregular, fan-shaped arrangement to a tight, close posy, where the individual shape of each supposedly carefully cut flower is lost by being hidden under another. A teacher should mark these exercises on two

46

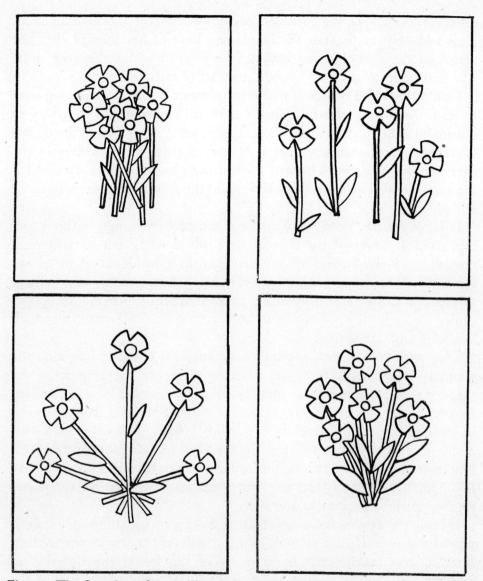

Fig. 10. The first three figures illustrate typical mistakes made by the children. The fourth figure shows satisfactory grouping

47

separate counts—on the cutting of the flowers and on their arrangement. This will help to prevent the child who has cut her flowers well but arranged them badly from making the same mistakes the next time. She will hope to get two 'Goods' instead of only one.

One of the chief causes of bad arrangement is that the children tend to stick the flowers down as they cut them, whereas, the only way to ensure good arrangement is not to stick anything down until the design is complete, for, once anything is affixed, there is no possibility of the necessary adjustment. The first part of the grouping to be attached is the stems, and when this has been done, the flowers and leaves can be added.

It is, of course, possible to make a satisfactory design without any stems visible amongst the flowers, and this must be left to individual choice; but if the flowers are not arranged in a pot, garland or 'swag' form, they seem to need this means of holding them together and helping to create a unity; and, moreover, stems frequently provide an opportunity for including a contrast of hue or tone in small quantity, which is useful and attractive.

The cutting of shapes in paper is definitely a craft, and as such the standard of manipulation should be rated highly. Consequently, the teacher who hurries on too quickly from the cutting of four-petalled flowers to other varieties, regardless of the care which is being taken in establishing a high standard of cutting, is being unwise, for once the children have become careless, it would seem almost impossible to eradicate this quality. It is better for the work to be stopped completely for a time, and even then the first freshness has worn off when one returns to the attack at a later date.

Having cut circles and four-petalled flowers in a first lesson, I should repeat this exercise in a second, giving a different colour to provide new interest, but making the main point of the lesson the question of arrangement. Since teaching of cutting has already been done in the first lesson, and the second will only be revision, this part of the lesson

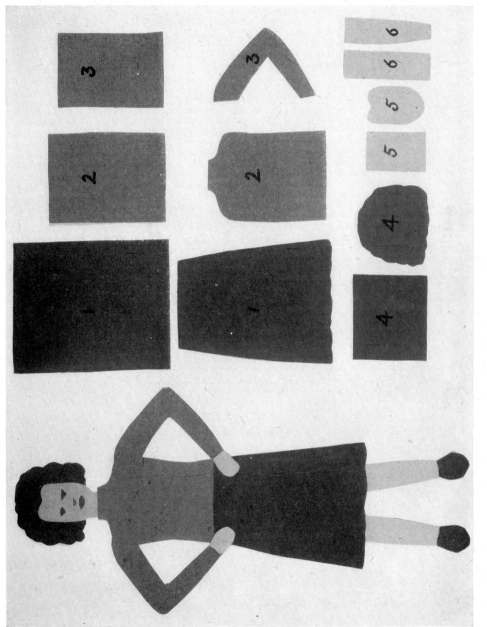

XVII. Figure Cutting, by C. R. Cox

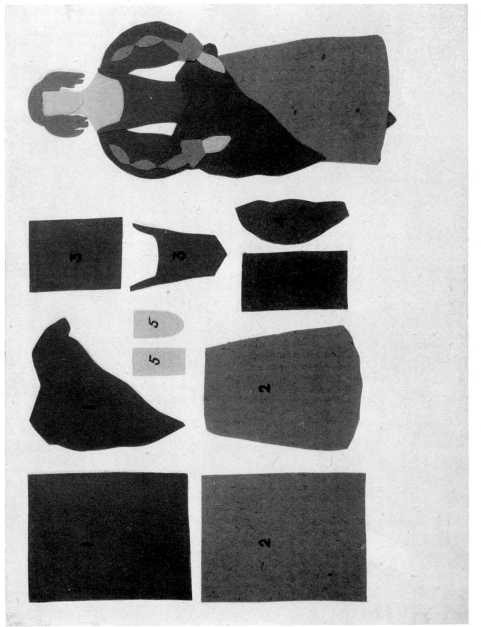

XVIII. Figure Cutting, by C. R. Cox

should proceed more quickly than in the previous case, and the question of arrangement be arrived at sooner.

Then the teacher, by pinning up good, bad, and indifferent arrangements from the children's work, can proceed to make her points, of which one should be that, having taken trouble to cut nice shapes, one should arrange them so that those shapes show to good advantage, and another that, when shapes are grouped together, that group has a shape of its own which is very obvious and must, therefore, be nice to look at (see Fig. 10). After this discussion on arrangement, the teacher can, if she likes, either let the children arrange their second lot of flowers which they have just cut, and see what effect the talk has had, or she can decide to let the whole class carry out one form of arrangement which she suggests, or she can put up a number of suggested arrangements on the board and let the children choose individually which of them they would like to do best (see Fig. 11, Nos. 2 to 5).

There is a lot to be said for either of the two latter methods, if used judiciously. More, I think, than for the first, perhaps, because one can only express oneself in a material according to one's personal experience, and, judging that in many cases this is extremely slight, it is the experience which one wants to expand by learning different possibilities of arrangement. A teacher must always beware, however, if she dictates how she wishes a thing to be done, that she does not destroy the initiative of her class; and, having let the children produce examples of different arrangements to her instructions in, say, two subsequent lessons, she should next allow them scope for entire freedom of choice and judgement before she makes them too reliant on her guidance.

When the children have learnt to cut different shapes of flowers, and to make these of different sizes according to the choice of predominant colour, the question of arrangement becomes both more interesting and more complicated because, not only does one have to consider arranging the flowers so that their individual shapes show to advantage, and so that the shape of the group is attractive, but also so that the

49

pattern of the colour is well balanced throughout the group. Arrangements can fall into two categories: those which are informal in their plan but which are balanced by the relative weights of colour and sizes of flowers, as in Plate III; and those which are actually symmetrical and depend on the regular distribution of shapes and colours, as in Plate IV.

Of the two, the latter is by far the simpler method, and since it develops the sensitiveness to balance which is essential to the production of successful non-symmetrical treatment, it provides very valuable experience. This sensitiveness to balance can only develop gradually by means of experience; and cut paper, since the shapes are movable and do not present the necessity of 'rubbing out and beginning again', is an excellent medium for aiding such development.

The problems I have dealt with are general ones, and embrace the difficulties of general class treatment in the earlier stages of this work. As the shapes used by children become greater in number, variety and colour, problems become more individual, and because, if no limit is set, the work can get too complicated and fussy, I advise that, on embarking on a fresh piece of work, the teacher should make the children individually select say not more than three types of flower for their study, with the corresponding number of colours, and extend to four on another occasion as experience in manipulation develops.

A certain amount of limitation in this way on the part of the teacher does not prevent the work from being individual—rather it prevents the work from being uncontrolled.

In designing decoration for an object which is going to be used, the practical purpose of the object acts as a brake to the disposition of the decoration. In a medium such as cut paper, where the end is to make a decoration which serves no practical purpose, there is no such limitation, and therefore it often keeps the mind livelier to have a definite problem to tackle—such as making a successful design from a limited number of colours, or to a definite pattern of arrangement—than it does to be entirely free.

50

CHAPTER VI

CO-OPERATIVE WORK

In the closing paragraphs of the chapter on work in the Infant and Lower Junior classes, I mentioned that co-operative work presented problems of its own with which I would deal elsewhere.

The first section of this chapter is devoted to the cutting of toys for co-operative decorations for the class-room—work which is suited to the interest and ability of the top infant and lower junior classes, as well as older children. The latter section, on co-operative floral decorations, is definitely intended for the upper junior and senior classes only, as this type of work requires more detailed teaching and more concentration than is either suitable or possible with younger children.

The co-operative lesson, in which each child in the class combines to make some part of a larger and more complicated decoration than can be easily accomplished individually, is one which calls for absolute understanding of purpose and careful organization on the part of the teacher.

In the first place, any kind of work undertaken co-operatively provides a very poor opportunity for individuality. It is essential, if a satisfactory piece of work is to be produced, for one mind to dominate the production, and the class, therefore, takes the position of factory hands whose job it is to produce the different parts of the manufactured article under the direction of a foreman.

This may sound as though I do not approve of co-operative work, but I have purposely stated my case strongly. I do approve of co-operative work providing that the teacher understands and recognizes how it can be introduced to serve both her own purpose of getting attractive decorations on a large scale for her class-room, and also that of repeating, with a fresh interest of purpose, the cutting of toys, flowers, or other shapes previously attempted which can benefit by repetition.

One thing she must realize, and this is that a co-operative lesson is not one in which it is wise to attempt the introduction of fresh constructive problems. All the teacher's energies should be free to concentrate on the organization of the lesson, so that, firstly, everyone has plenty to do and, secondly, she can see that suitable work is given to the different groups of the class. The brighter children should be kept busy doing the more complicated work, the simpler work being left for the more backward children.

TOY CUTTING

Decoration of Christmas trees at a seasonable period, and filling shelves of a toy shop, provide attractive subject matter in this field. Here I would repeat the same advice as I have given in the Introduction to this chapter: do not embark on a subject which is a fresh experience at the same time as you organize a co-operative lesson—let the children gain some experience in previous lessons, where they cut individual pictures of the toys. These toys should be displayed one at a time, so that the children may learn how to tackle the cutting of each individual shape which goes to the making up of the whole, and then carefully assemble the separate pieces and stick them down.

These individual pieces of work should be kept in the children's folders, and receive the same respect as any other artistic effort.

When they have learnt to tackle the cutting of such toys as crackers, a cricket bat and ball, a ship, a Noah's ark, a gollywog, a dolls' house, and any others which present definite and easily identified shapes, the co-operative lesson can be embarked on.

One of the reasons why I write so definitely on this point is because I have tried both ways of working in this respect. I have tried letting the children cut toys for a christmas tree straightaway and without previous exercise and experience, and I have tried the same subject prefaced by three or four lessons in which the cutting of individual toys has been done by the whole class.

In each case the children certainly enjoyed the work, but the first case was not comparable with the latter either in artistic or psychological result. The excitement of decorating the trees was intense, and it was almost impossible to get the children to look at the toys with any care at all—one glance and they were off, cutting rapidly, and, although the toys they cut were recognizable, the carelessness in the cutting was equally so!

In the latter case, experience of cutting toys was given first in previous lessons. To take an instance of this method, we will say that a ship shall be the first subject, and this put up in a position in which the whole class can see it. 'Now, supposing you were making this ship, what do you think would be the first part you would make?' The main part of the boat having been agreed on, a discussion will then take place as to what shaped piece of wood would be needed from which to cut this shape, and an oblong decided on. This oblong will then be cut, and the necessary adjustments made, probably in rough paper first and then in coloured paper, after which the masts can be cut, and then the sails.

In a lesson such as this, an individual child may want to put some sea underneath the boat, or a sailor on board the ship, and this should certainly not be discouraged. The children should be allowed to make their work as individual as possible.

When enough experience has been gained for the children to be capable of working on their own without need of much assistance or advice, the teacher can prepare a co-operative lesson. One possibility is always a frieze, and may I suggest here that black is by no means the only suitable background for such a subject—blue or a neutral fawn is equally suitable and more attractive, being less startling. The whole assembly of toys which the children have been cutting can then be put out in front of the class, and the children can choose which toy they individually would most like to do. It is easier, of course, as they want to have the toy available, to let the children sit together who choose one particular toy, so that they do not have to move about to see it.

In the assembling and sticking down of the toys, the cut shapes can be laid out, unattached, on the frieze, which should be placed horizontally in some available place. If there are too many toys for all of them to be used, the best ones can be voted on by the children and selected, and according to the variation of types of toys the arrangement will differ and can be agreed on between class and teacher.

With regard to the shop window, several methods can be adopted. One of my students prepared a large card which was divided by coloured strips into separate panes. Each child in the class had a pane, and put into that little window just what toys he or she wanted. In this method, however, care must be taken not to get the window panes too small, for cut paper work is essentially a type of work which should be done on a large scale.

The student used the individual window panes and their contents as material for her arithmetic lesson after their completion. Each toy was priced, and the value of the stock arrived at by addition, and multiplication sums were provided by ordering a further stock of some individual toy.

In the case of the larger shop window, such as the one included amongst my illustrations (see Plate VI), and also the Christmas tree (see Plate XIII), the teacher should supply the necessary background, since it involves so many difficulties with the class and uses up time which can be better and more individually employed elsewhere. The long strips of paper required for window frames and shelves require careful manipulation or they become very messy and untidy.

May I give one word of helpful warning to the teacher who is embarking on the preparation of a cut-out Christmas tree? My first attempt was a lamentable failure because I made the mistake of damping the whole tree all at once, and the side branches immediately rolled themselves up and stuck themselves firmly on to the middle of

54

the tree. The next time I damped the centre portion of the tree, as far as the beginning of the branches, and having fixed this in position, I used a damp paintbrush with which to moisten each branch in turn and stick it down. This method was entirely satisfactory, and the trees in their tubs look sufficiently attractive, when they are prepared, to arouse the enthusiasm of any class in the top infant or junior school, and certainly these co-operative efforts make splendid decorations for class-room walls.

I have never forgotten the transforming effect of a cut paper frieze in a dingy class-room in one of the old-fashioned slum schools in Birmingham, and anyone whose room needs brightening up need have no hesitation in experimenting with this gay and attractive material.

FLORAL PAPER CUTTING

When I started doing floral cut paper work and wanted to make a co-operative decoration, I remembered the local custom at my home in the country of making garlands on May Day, and their suitability as a subject struck me.

Recalling that the children's garlands were always made on a green foundation of moss, I provided a green circle for the class, and allotted the cutting of the flowers and leaves to different people, and the result is shown in Plate IX.

The formality of arrangement necessary for obtaining a good decorative effect in a garland can be compared with the natural laws which underlie the making of patterns.

The simplest type of garland could be made of flowers all of one size arranged in regular repeat form (see Fig. 12), but in order to make a really interesting effect, varieties in the sizes and types of flowers, and different colours and spacings, must make their appearance (see Fig. 11, No. (2), and Plate IX).

If the chapter on colour is read with reference to the Plate illustrating this chapter, it will be seen that what I have said about a dominant

55

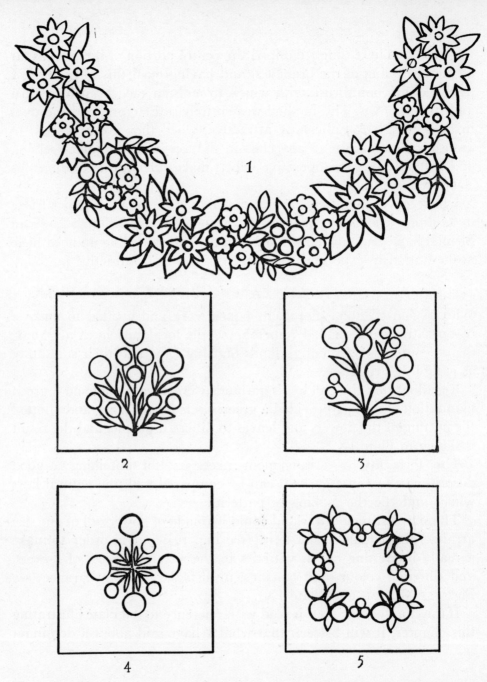

Fig. 11. (1) Swag arrangement, which can be continued in loops to form a frieze. (2) Symmetrical arrangement. (3) Balancing arrangement. (4) Formal symmetrical arrangement. (5) Ditto

56

XIX. 'Persephone', by B. P. Walton

XX. 'The Wheatsheaf Inn', by M. F. Wainwright

colour scheme relieved by contrast of hue is obvious here. The main colour scheme is yellow to red orange, and it is relieved by small blue and purple flowers. Another point which is very obvious is the variety of size and type of flower. In order to ensure that the correct proportion was adopted, each student was given a circle of the size of the flower required, and shown to which type of flower shape it was to be reduced.

When the flower and leaf shapes had all been cut, a discussion took place as to how these could be arranged, and the form agreed on tried out, but nothing was stuck down until the complete arrangement had been made.

I have tried making garlands co-operatively with groups of students, with one student responsible for organizing each group, but I generally find that, unless they are very gifted in design, they tend to miss these points of the value of variety of size and type of flower, and it is necessary to take a lesson illustrating these facts before embarking on the choice of flowers and their cutting. Without guidance, the tendency is to choose too many types of flower and too much detail, and the effect is fussy and lacking in unity. The ideal way is always to learn by experience rather than by theory, and with children I should prefer to work on the lines of directing different types of arrangement in different lessons (and so giving variety of experience first), and then let the children sum up the knowledge they have gained by reference to these different arrangements before they embark on a similar exercise independent of the teacher's direction.

I feel sure that this is much more enjoyable to the children than a previous discussion on possible forms of arrangement when they are anxious to start working, and it greatly adds to the interest and fun in making garlands when they discover, through experience, these possibilities which they had not previously realized.

The 'swag' arrangement of continuous loops of flowers is a very pleasant decoration for a class-room wall (see Fig. 11, No. (1)), and this,

Fig. 12. (1) Repeat arrangement of flowers all same size and shape but alternating colours of flowers and centres. (2) Alteration in arrangements using two shapes and sizes of flowers, and alternating colour. For further developed garland, see coloured plate

too, has very different possibilities according to the different sizes and number of the various flowers.

The bowl of flowers can be much less formal in arrangement than the garland or the swag, and still prove effective, because the subject itself seems to demand less formality. Here the teacher will provide the bowl and the children cut the different types of flowers in varying sizes to fit in with the colour scheme (see Plate XVI).

A flower border presents another possible arrangement (see Plate XIV), and a strip of brown for soil and of green for grass can help in the decorative effect—the brown will show between the smaller flowers at the bottom of the border, and the green is not only decorative but practical in covering up the junctures of stems and leaves, etc., whilst,

58

from the point of view of composition, the long lines of brown and green echo the form of the frieze and help to give unity and decorative effect.

The frieze included in this book is made of flowers cut from nature, which is quite possible when sufficient experience has been gained in the selecting and cutting of typical forms. A frieze can be equally successful made from conventional flowers—it rests purely on the suitability of shapes, their relative size and colour, and their arrangement.

In organizing this lesson, the brown strip for the soil should be stuck on to the background first, and the flowers arranged over this. The border of grass is the last part to be stuck down, and can be varied in width according to necessity. So much, then, for a brief discussion on the possibilities of co-operative floral decorations.

CHAPTER VII

FIGURE CUTTING, ETC.

HAVING dealt extensively and in detail with the cutting of floral shapes and the decorative possibilities of their arrangement, it seems only necessary that some consideration should be given to the problems of cutting figures and the other objects such as houses, animals, trees, etc., which generally furnish the subject matter in pictorial work. Here the problems are somewhat different, for although it is perfectly possible to take an ideal flower type, and use it with interest and variety by altering its size and colour, it is an entirely different proposition to take a figure type and try to repeat it in the same manner.

I think it would be generally agreed that to teach figure cutting by a process of reducing the forms to type would be a very bad thing indeed, for one's appreciation of figure subjects is instinctively influenced by the human interest which gives life and character to the work.

If one looks at Plate XV, of figures made by children in the infant school, it is obvious that these have been built up of a number of shapes, or crude symbols for these shapes—a head and neck, body, arms and legs.

With older children one can naturally develop a much more sensitive appreciation of refinements of form than is possible with infants and young juniors, and in just the same way as it is possible to do this by teaching them to draw from a figure model, so is it possible to teach them to cut from one. In fact, I have found that students who were quite incapable of drawing a figure succeed perfectly well with scissors and paper.

One thing, however, must be remembered by the teacher, and that is that the pose of the model must, of necessity, give good comprehensible shapes. Three-quarter views frequently present extremely

60

difficult problems of foreshortening which are far too complicated to tackle convincingly until one has capably studied back, front, and side views. Character, after all, is one of the most interesting parts of figure study, and a succession of models in the same position helps one to realize how different individuals look under similar circumstances.

The shape of the face, varying from a round oval to a long rounded rectangular shape—of the hair lying sleek to the head with neat orderly fringe, or framing the face in a turbulent mass which rivals the shoulders in its extent of width—the long thin body with rather high waist and long thin legs—the short, tubby body with firm, shapely legs—the square shoulders, drooping shoulders, rounded shoulders— all these characteristic features can be shown to perfection in the forms of a cut-out figure built up of a succession of shapes which are put together piece by piece, just as one does a jig-saw puzzle.

The easiest method of procedure is to decide on the part of the figure which is definitely the largest in proportion to the whole. This is, generally, either the dress shape, if this is all in one piece, or the length from waist to hem, if a jumper and skirt is worn, or the legs, but I should advise beginning with the largest dress shape in preference to the legs, as it is easier to do so.

A rectangle should then be cut of suitable proportion of width to height, and this shape reduced to that of the dress or skirt of the model.

Following on this another rectangle is cut, proportionately smaller than the first, and from this the next part of the body is cut, and so on.

The method of procedure will probably be better understood by studying the diagrams which accompany this chapter (see Plate XVII).

Historical costume provides splendid opportunity for decorative figure study, and paper cutting shows to full advantage the varying silhouettes provided by the different clothes of different periods (see Plate XVIII).

Interest in the structural methods of paper cutting can be stimulated, e.g. by a discussion of the most suitable shape from which to cut a

E

crinoline skirt compared with an Early Victorian one, or an Elizabethan and a Georgian.

In connection with figures in period costume, houses of the period can also be studied from photographs, their proportionate width compared with their height, and outstanding details such as half-timbering in early Tudor work, and the regular disposition of rectangular sash windows in the Georgian house can be successfully used with decorative effect.

It is impossible to deal with the enormous variety of subject matter which pictorial work entails, and this makes it all the more clear that it is the method of approach which is important.

Once the children have grasped the principle of seizing on outstanding characteristics, and of comparing and contrasting the shapes and proportions of the various parts which go to make up the whole, they will begin to progress in the decorative use of their material.

Lessons which have as their subject matter the cutting of specific things such as figures, either in period or modern dress, houses, animals, etc., help a great deal in providing inspiration for pictorial work, and deal with problems which will be met there in just the same way as preliminary toy cutting broadens the experience and lessens the difficulties of using this material in a co-operative lesson.

CHAPTER VIII

PICTURE MAKING

COMPARED with the problems we have been discussing in preceding chapters, the manipulation of materials, formal methods of cutting symmetrical shapes, practical methods of considering things which are a combination of shapes, questions of arrangement, and so forth, the making of a picture in coloured paper is quite a different matter. All pictures contain an essentially personal element which is the result either of direct inspiration or of individual additions to a nucleus subject which has been provided by an outside person. To put this a little more clearly, in order to make a picture, not merely a decoration with floral shapes or toys, which one can cut out before one has decided on their eventual arrangement, one needs an inspiration or an idea. The word idea is a watered-down version of the former term, because it implies the term subject matter, but not the combination of subject plus understanding of material which the word inspiration implies.

If one has an inspiration for a cut paper picture, the particular qualities of cut paper work—the boldness and simplicity of its character —are either consciously or unconsciously the means of promoting the idea of the picture. If the limitations imposed by the material—the need for simplicity and lack of fine detail—are not accepted and recognized, then one could carry out one's idea far better with pencils and paints, for it is an idea but it has not been inspired by this particular material with its very definite limitations.

The types of pictures which result from this kind of approach are obviously extremely individual, and only a few people are capable of producing them (see Plates XIX and XX). They are the people who can appreciate and understand the natural qualities of a material, and think in terms of these—in fact, draw their inspiration from them. For this type of person the provision of a subject is generally unnecessary; they will provide their own, but only when inspiration comes, and then they should be allowed to express themselves without interference.

On the other hand a subject may be given which has the effect of stirring up a desire for expression, and this would be the more general way, perhaps, of dealing with an inexperienced class. A subject such as 'a girl picking flowers', or 'a nice house and garden', or an abstract title like 'spring', could be used to encourage the flow of inspiration.

Two methods could be adopted in attempting to start people making pictures in coloured paper. One would be to make it compulsory in one lesson for everybody to use scissors and paper, and in later lessons relax from this and give a choice of either paints or paper, if the latter medium proved not universally popular. The other method would be to let people choose which medium they would prefer from the start with no compulsion in favour of either.

In the first instance timid people, who would probably not venture on such an enterprise unless a problem were put directly into their hands, might find that they could produce something which previously they had not thought possible, and so benefit thereby; whilst in the latter case the lack of restraint and freedom to choose materials can have a very beneficial result in developing independence and individuality; while seeing other people using materials which one has not tried oneself is a sure way of producing an appetite for doing so, be it curiosity alone which prompts the desire to experiment.

In making a picture in any material, although problems of representation are perhaps the greatest difficulties to be met with, those of composition are much more important.

The word composition is, I think, a frightening one to most people. They hear artists or connoisseurs talking about the laws of composition, and what had previously seemed to them a plain and simple picture suddenly becomes full of mysteries of which they feel they are neither conscious nor appreciative.

64

What everyone is capable of appreciating, however, if they bother to use their eyes, is that no picture, no matter how well drawn, is pleasing if shapes are littered about in it without any order, and without consideration for the scale of the space they occupy.

A picture should make its meaning plain, which it does through the grouping of the shapes within the chosen space.

This instinct for making a pattern develops much more quickly than the ability to represent. A child of five, when making a picture, will instinctively fill up empty spaces whilst he is incapable of representing things except by the crudest possible symbols. Unfortunately, however, due to misunderstanding on the part of his teachers and lack of appreciation of its true value, this instinct for making good patterns of his pictures is apt to be pushed to one side for what we Westerners tend to think is the more important content of a picture—the representational side.

The average teacher will get much more excited over a child's work which is representationally advanced, albeit the pattern of the picture is poor, than he will over a crude effort in which the arrangement shows real sensitiveness for good pattern. Plate X, which is the work of a child of 7+, shows how attractive a sensitive arrangement of colour can be without the addition of highly developed skill in representation.

We are, however, in this respect, largely the victims of our upbringing, and of whatever so-called art education we have received, which, in the majority of cases, has taught us to assume that anyone who can draw is an artist, and that the artist's job is to portray what he sees.

One of the things which cramps a child's ideas of arrangement in making his picture is, I am sure, the teacher's determination to make him represent the ground and the sky by two masses of green and blue.

The contents of a child's early pictures have no spatial relationship, and he does not represent either ground or sky. He is free to fill his page as he likes, and consequently concentrates on filling it, but once

65

he has been instructed, as frequently happens in some schools, to divide his picture into halves, and colour one part green and one part blue, to represent earth and sky, the possibility of any originality in the disposition of his shapes is seriously hampered by these solid masses of colour which seem to dwarf the importance of anything else. What I always say to people who dispute this point with me is that in all the other departures of a child's artistic work one is forced to accept its symbolic character and his inability to express himself in other than symbolic form. Why, then, should one pick on one fact, such as the ground meeting the sky, and make it of any more importance than the fact that a man's head is not round, and that his limbs cannot be represented by two straight lines?

I think the reason for this attitude is, firstly, that it is one of the ideas left over from the old school of thought which did not believe in the legitimacy of a child's expressing himself in his own natural way, but had to tell him how to do everything, and secondly, alas, because it is such an easy thing to teach!

I think that my readers may think that I have not said anything very definite about how cut paper pictures can be made. This has been deliberate on my part, for I feel that it is impossible to teach people to make pictures by means of rules and instructions, whether they be in cut paper or any other material. Sir Joshua Reynolds' remark, 'Rules are made from pictures, not pictures from rules', holds good whether the material be crayon, pencil, paints or coloured paper.

What I have tried to make clear in this chapter, however, is the attitude which a teacher should adopt towards her class and its efforts, so that she will not think that ready-made recipes for making pictures are either possible or desirable.

Over practical issues she can certainly help, and one of these is that when cut paper is chosen as the medium for representation, she can see that no other medium is used with it.

The desire for detail which prompts a child to add pencilled eyes and

66

nose and mouth to his cut paper picture can be satisfied by encouraging him to make his figure larger so that these details can be added in coloured paper instead (see Plate X). The teacher can make an example of two figures, one showing the decorative effect of detail carried out in coloured paper, and the other the faintness and ineffectuality of detail in another medium. It can be pointed out how the boldness of the cut paper picture makes it show up from a distance, whereas the pencil detail is too delicate to stand side by side with such a strong companion.

I find that children are very reasonable in this respect. I once asked some children of ten who had made a cut paper picture with a number of pencilled details if they would make me one all in coloured paper. 'Oh yes,' said one girl promptly, 'but we shall have to make it bigger.' Obviously, then, unless it is possible to carry out the work on a very big scale, or unless one is willing to eliminate detail—which is often the product of a more sophisticated appreciation of the medium (e.g. Plates XIX and XX) than a child is likely to produce—it is unwise to choose as subjects for the pictures those which demand the inclusion of a number of things.

I said in the early part of this chapter that a nucleus subject provided by an outside person could help to start the flow of inspiration, and I meant by this that once the main interest of the picture had been established by pinning the importance to one thing—a little girl in her best frock, for instance, or a girl picking flowers—other details could be added entirely individually to complete the picture.

It is advisable to indicate to the children that they should make their figure as large as the paper will comfortably allow, and this goes far towards helping them to consider the filling of the shape and to allow for the inclusion of detail.

Another practical point on which the teacher needs to stand firm is to see that nothing is stuck down on the background until everything for the picture is complete. As I have remarked before, one of the great advantages of cut paper is that until it is attached one can move

67

it about and alter the arrangement to suit oneself. Equally so, its disadvantage is that once stuck down it cannot be erased, so that any additional background must be stuck down first and the contents of the picture put on top of this.

Probably the wise teacher will let her class make the possible mistake at least once, so that it is fixed in their minds as an experience rather than a warning.

The teacher's part in this type of lesson, therefore, as I hope I have made clear, should be very much the same as in any other art lesson where she is aiming at giving the children opportunity for expression. (She should provide materials and organize their distribution, create an atmosphere of enthusiasm for the work in hand, and, having set the class to work, be ready to give the benefit of her interest, encouragement, and experience when it is needed. She need not teach the children to make a picture. That, when they are capable of manipulating their scissors and paper without being worried by them, they will do for themselves.)

The entire treatment, therefore, of this type of lesson is different from that in which one is teaching how to cut formal flower shapes or toys. In doing this one is opening the eyes to the beauty of symmetrical shapes and teaching the manipulation of materials in order to produce this beauty of shape. The making of a picture need not employ such able control of material, for the shapes employed are much more free in character. As soon as a child is capable of using his scissors to cut with some control, he is capable of producing a picture of sorts (see Plate V), and whereas formal exercises such as some of those described in previous chapters would be unsuitable by reason of their demanding too much concentration power and manipulative control, the making of pictures in which no formal teaching is involved can provide him with much enjoyment. Coloured cut paper work is, however, definitely not the choice of every child, and if other materials are preferred, the desire to use them in preference should not be thwarted.

68

CHAPTER IX

SUGGESTED PLANS FOR LESSONS

THIS chapter has been written with the aim of helping people who are inexperienced in teaching to see how they can plan their lessons with a definite aim, and develop one lesson from the experience gained in the previous lesson, plus the addition of some further experience and interest, in order to cultivate, side by side, the powers of manipulation and of sensitiveness to beauty of effect.

As in every case when lessons are planned apart from a particular class, they would need to be modified according to the age of the children, the duration of the lesson, and the rate at which the children work, but by showing how each lesson can provide a possible basis for the aim of the next lesson, I hope I have made clear the principle of progressive teaching. If a class is quick and bright and skilful with materials they would probably cut both four- and eight-petalled flowers in the first lesson, and the second lesson could proceed to the decoration of the eight-petalled flowers by cutting indentations, plus the further interest of discussion of arrangement, and more difficult flower shapes, such as the pointed petalled and the rounded petalled flowers, can be introduced as skill develops in succeeding lessons.

As I have remarked in the chapter on flower cutting, it is unwise to go on to more difficult flowers if the cutting of the simple ones is poor, and if the children enjoy the paper cutting but find the flowers difficult to do, it would be much wiser to cut toys, where the shapes are larger and less intricate, or to make pictures based on one large subject such as a house or a figure, so that the scale is kept large.

The repetition in a co-operative lesson of the exercises done in previous lessons gives opportunity for revision plus the fresh interest of making a different kind of picture, and when used with discretion can be beneficial to both children and teacher, or the results provide very effective large-scale decorations for the class-room, in addition to the fresh experience.

I

AIM OF LESSON

    (*a*) To teach children to cut circles and make them into flowers with four petals.

    (*b*) To let each child make a small posy.

APPARATUS

    For Children

    (*a*) Newspaper for each child, scissors, two coloured papers for the flowers, green for leaves and stems, background paper, envelope.

    (*b*) Stiff paper for demonstration use.

    For Teacher

    Small posy, such as children can make, as attractively arranged as possible.

METHOD

The children spread out the newspaper on their desks. This is to act partially as a preventative to untidiness, and partially for use for experiment. All materials being provided, and children ready to start, the teacher holds up a circle cut out of paper, and asks the children to cut her a circle from a piece of their newspaper.

Whilst they are doing this she can go round and note the methods adopted. Generally these are of two types: by means of folding (see Fig. 4, page 39) and by free cutting into the paper without any guiding shape.

Having let the children experiment, the teacher can stop them and demonstrate, if necessary, the cutting of a circle from a square by means

70

of rounding off the corners (Fig. 5). The children then cut squares and cut circles from them.

Teacher should look out for tendency to miss the point of the use of the square by cutting into it (see Fig. 6) and correct this by a blackboard drawing and second demonstration of cutting if necessary.

When children can cut circles reasonably well, they can repeat the exercise in coloured paper.

The teacher can now show the posy of flowers she has made, and ask the children if they would like to make flowers of their circles.

(The demonstration picture should not be left up on the wall, but merely shown to arouse enthusiasm.)

The children then experiment with their newspaper circles, cutting four petals, followed, if necessary, by a demonstration by the teacher, who stresses unsuitability of folding on account of spoiling the look of the paper.

The children try this in their rough paper, if necessary, and then in coloured paper. Emphasis should be put on pointing the scissors towards the centre of the circle when cutting the guide slits for petal division, or the circle will not be divided evenly (see Fig. 9).

Smaller circles can be cut out of the other coloured paper and added as centres to the flowers.

The children can then cut some stalks and leaves from their green paper. The teacher then suggests that the children should imagine that they have picked these flowers to give to someone, and that they want them to look as nice as possible, so they must arrange them carefully.

She then leaves them to make their own arrangement in their own way. (The arranging and sticking down generally takes quite ten minutes, and this should be allowed for in the time allotted for the lesson.)

The children then place any flowers they have not used, or small scraps of coloured paper, in their envelope, on which they put their

71

names. Larger pieces of coloured paper are collected up, and all the small odds and ends are rolled up in the newspaper and put into the waste-paper basket.

II

AIM OF LESSON

(*a*) To develop children's appreciation for good arrangement.

(*b*) To repeat work of former lesson with interest of different colour, and, if time, to teach cutting of eight-petalled flower.

APPARATUS

For Children

Same as last lesson, with different colours provided.

For Teacher

Examples of best arrangement from children's work, and one or two examples where the flowers have been bunched too close together or too far apart.

METHOD

Teacher asks children to cut a flower, like the one they cut before, from their newspaper, to show if they have remembered. Then, if necessary, she can revise any points forgotten, and children can then cut their four-petalled flowers out of coloured paper.

Teacher then shows the class an eight-petalled flower and asks how they think it was cut.

E.g. How many petals are there? How many divisions in circle?

Children cut eight-petalled flower. (As the main aim of the lesson is arrangement rather than teaching the cutting of a fresh shape, this can be omitted if time is short, and leaves and stems cut instead.)

When flowers, stems, and leaves are cut, the teacher can pin up the examples illustrating good and indifferent arrangement, and ask the children why some look nicer than others.

The two points she wants to stress are that the flowers which they have taken care in cutting must not have their shapes spoilt by crowding on top of one another (see Fig. 10 (top left)), or those shapes are lost, and if they are placed too far apart they do not look nice (see Fig. 10 (top right and bottom left)), so they must space their flowers carefully before they stick them down.

Another point which will probably need calling attention to is that the stalks need sticking down before the flowers, or the joins look unpleasant (see Fig. 10 (top right)). The children then arrange and stick down their stems and flowers and leaves, and clear up odd pieces of paper.

III

Aim of Lesson

(a) To show how variation of size of flower adds to the attraction of the effect of an arrangement of floral shapes.

(b) Opportunity for revision of previous work with fresh interest.

Apparatus

For Children

Same as previous lessons, with provision of different colours.

For Teacher

(a) One example of four- and eight-petalled flowers with flowers both the same size.

(b) An example with eight-petalled flowers larger than four-petalled ones.

(Care must be taken to make the second illustration more attractive than the first.) (See Plate XII.)

Method

Teacher shows the two examples and asks which looks the more attractive. Why is the second example more attractive than the first?

In order to get the flowers of two sizes the children cut a large square and also one of a smaller size, which are reduced to circles, and then the larger one to eight petals, and the smaller to four. If time, the eight-petalled flower may be decorated by cutting a 'V' shape from the centre of each petal.

The children then arrange and stick down their work.

IV

AIM OF LESSON

To make a co-operative garland or bowl or frieze of flowers, using the shapes cut in the last three lessons, and variations of size of flower.

APPARATUS

Squares of three sizes cut out of rough paper sufficient in number to go round the class, each child to have one square with the exception of those who are to cut leaves. Three harmonizing coloured papers, green for leaves (unless another colour is preferred). Scissors, rough paper, etc. Large sheets of paper for backgrounds.

METHOD

Teacher tells children that they are going to join together to make big garlands (or whatever grouping is decided on), which they will make from the different flowers they have learnt to cut.

Do they remember what they learnt last lesson? (Variety of size makes picture more interesting.)

She refers to the three sizes of squares which have been given out, and, if wise, she will see that the largest squares for the largest flowers are given to the more skilful children. These will have eight petals and can be decorated with a 'V'-shaped cut.

The next size of square will be plain eight-petalled, and the four-petalled flowers, which are smallest of all, and the leaves can be cut by the people who find the work most difficult.

This part of the lesson can proceed as usual, the children having been told to cut squares of the same sizes as their rough-paper ones in coloured paper, and then make circles of them.

When all the material for the garlands is ready, the teacher will divide the class into groups, each group containing children who have cut decorated eight-petalled flowers, plain eight-petalled flowers, four-petalled flowers, and leaves, which will be collected into four piles. She can then elect a captain who will be responsible for the order and control of each group. The children will then be told to arrange their flowers as they think will look nice.

If garlands are being done, it is advisable for the teacher to put guide rings on the background papers to help unity of shape. If bowls of flowers are being done, the bowls will be provided by the teacher, ready stuck down.

The children should be allowed to use their own ideas, and if the results show little sense of arrangement, a further lesson may be taken after a reasonable interval in which the aim is to make the children conscious of possible arrangement. This could be done by showing examples of different groupings, and letting the children choose which one they would like to make.

In every case in planning practical lessons, the teacher should see that she does not talk at length at any one period of the lesson. Problems should be tackled by discussion as the lesson proceeds, and class experiment should always precede demonstration.

These lessons are only specimens illustrating this principle. I hope they will prove helpful in directing people who have difficulties in planning their lessons.